The future is digital:
A blueprints to success

Author: Aliyu Yahya Dorayi

Copyright © 2023 Aliyu Yahya Dorayi. All rights reserved. No part of this publication may be reproduced, distributed, or transmitted in any form or by any means, including photocopying, recording, or other electronic or mechanical methods, without the prior written permission of the publisher, except in the case of brief quotations embodied in critical reviews and certain other noncommercial uses permitted by copyright law. For permission requests, write to the publisher, addressed

"Attention: Permissions Coordinator," at the following email address: aliyuyahyadorayi@gmail.com.

- **Acknowledgement**

I would like to extend a special thank you to Professor Isa Ali Pantami, the

Nigerian Minister of Communication and Digital Economy, for his contributions to

The digital economy in Nigeria. His leadership and expertise have been

Instrumental in promoting the growth of the digital sector in the country.

I would also like to acknowledge the benefits of changing money notes in a country, including

Improved security, increased efficiency, economic stimulation, modernization, and increased

Accessibility. These benefits are an important aspect of a country's progress and demonstrate

Its commitment to financial stability and economic development.

Finally, I would like to thank my readers for taking the time to read this book. I hope that it

Provides you with valuable insights and inspiration for your own journey in the digital world.

- **About The Author**

Aliyu Yahya Aliyu is a student of Computer Engineering Technology at Kano State

Polytechnic. With a passion for technology and a desire to expand his knowledge,

Aliyu has enrolled in a variety of online courses in computer science and related

Fields, including computational thinking, computer vision, mathematics for

Machine learning, and mathematical thinking.

Through his studies and practical experience, Aliyu has developed a deep understanding of the

Digital world and a strong commitment to staying up-to-date with the latest developments and

Trends in the field. He brings this expertise to his writing, offering readers a unique perspective

On the future of technology and the opportunities and challenges it presents.

With his background in computer engineering and his ongoing studies, Aliyu is well-equipped to

Help readers understand and navigate the complex world of digital technology. His book,

"Future is Digital: A Blueprint to Success," is a testament to his passion for technology and his

Commitment to sharing his knowledge and insights with others.

Content

Introduction
A. What is Digitalization?
B. Why it's important to use Digitalization
C. What this book is about

Chapter 1. Good Things about Digitalization
A. Work gets done faster
B. Customers are happier
C. Better way to collect and use data
D. Easier to work with others
E. Information and services are easier to access

Chapter 2. How Digitalization Changes Business
A. Businesses work differently
B. Businesses become more successful
C. Businesses make more money
D. Businesses run smoother
E. Businesses become more creative and flexible

Chapter 3. Using Digitalization in Your Business or Group
A. Make a plan for using digital tools

    B. Find the parts of your business that can be improved with digitalization
    C. Start using digital tools
    D. Make sure everyone is on board with digitalization
    E. Help people adjust to the changes

Chapter 4. Real-Life Examples of Digitalization Success
    A. Big companies
    B. Small businesses
    C. Groups that help people
    D. Government offices

Chapter 5. Problems and Risks with Digitalization
    A. Safety and privacy
    B. Technical difficulties
    C. People don't like change
    D. Finding and keeping good digital workers

Conclusion
    I. The Future of Digitalization
    I. Keep learning and adapting

Iii. Final thoughts and suggestions

Assalamu Alaikum Wa'rahmatul-lahi Ta'aalaa Wa'bara'kaatuhu.

- **Introduction**

. What is Digitalization?

Digitalization is using computers and the internet to do things. It helps us work faster, easier, and better. Instead of using paper and pen or doing things by hand, we use digital tools to get things done. This makes things more efficient and helps us save time.

For example, instead of going to the bank to deposit a check, you can take a picture of it with your phone and deposit it online. Instead of writing down a list of things to buy at the store, you can make a shopping list on your phone. Digitalization makes our lives easier and more convenient.

. Why it's important to use Digitalization?

1-

Saves time: Digital tools help us do things faster, so we have more time to do other things.

2-

Makes things easier: Digital tools are easy to use and make things more convenient.

3-

Improves customer service: Digitalization makes it easier for businesses to serve their customers, making them happier and more likely to come back.

4-

Helps with decision making: Digital tools help us collect and use data, so we can make better decisions.

5-

Better communication: Digitalization makes it easier to communicate and collaborate with others, no matter where they are.

6-

Gives access to information and services: With digitalization, we can easily access information and services online, making things more accessible.

7-

Increases productivity: Digital tools help us get more done in less time, making us more productive.

In short, digitalization makes our lives and work easier, faster, and better. That's why it's important to adopt and use digital tools.

• What this book is all about?

This book is about using digital tools to make things better. Digitalization is when we use computers and the internet to do things faster, easier, and better. It's important to learn about digitalization because it's changing the way we work, shop, and communicate.

In this book, you'll learn about the good things that come with digitalization and how it's changing the way businesses work. You'll also learn how to use digital tools in your own business or group, and see real examples of people who have already made the switch.

We'll talk about some of the challenges and risks that come with digitalization, but don't worry.
We'll also give you tips and suggestions for making the transition smooth and successful.

By the end of this book, you'll have a good understanding of what digitalization is and how it can help you and your organization. Let's get started!

Dedication statement

In conclusion, digitalization has become an integral part of our daily lives and is shaping the future of business and society. From small businesses to large corporations, digital tools are changing the way we work and communicate. While there are challenges to be faced, such as technical difficulties, privacy concerns, and resistance to change, the benefits of digitalization far outweigh these challenges. It is important to keep learning and adapting to these new technologies to stay ahead of the curve and make the most of these opportunities. This book, "Digitalization: Navigating the Future," written by Aliyu Yahya Dorayi, explores the world of digitalization and its impact on our lives. Dedicated to anyone who seeks to benefit from its contents, this book aims to provide insights, tips, and case studies to help you stay ahead in the digital age.

• What this book is about?

This book is about learning how to use tools to make things better. It covers the following topics:

The good things about digitalization and how it's changing the way we work.

How to use digital tools in your own business or group.

Real-life examples of people and organizations who have successfully adopted digitalization.

The challenges and risks that come with digitalization and how to overcome them.

Tips and suggestions for making the transition to digitalization smooth and successful. The goal of this book is to help you understand what digitalization is, why it's important, and how you can use it to improve your life and work. By the end of the book, you'll have a good understanding of how digitalization can help you and your organization.

• Chapter 1

Good things about digitalization!

1. Work get done faster

With digitalization, tasks that once required manual effort can now be automated, reducing the time and energy required to complete them. Digital tools also allow for realtime collaboration, which eliminates the need for manual coordination and speeds up decision-making processes. Additionally, digitalization provides access to vast amounts of data, which can be analyzed quickly and accurately to inform decisions and streamline processes. The result is increased efficiency and productivity, allowing work to get done faster. 2- **Customer are happier**

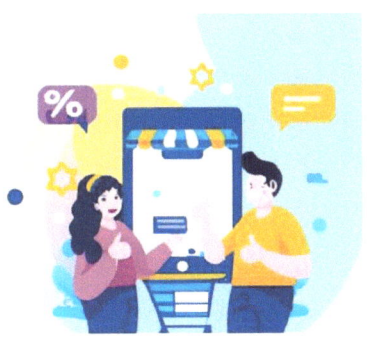

Customers are happier with digitalization because they can access information and services more easily and quickly. Digital tools make it easier for businesses to serve their customers, providing a better overall experience. For example, customers can now easily make purchases, access support, and track their orders online, without the need for in-person interactions or phone calls. Digitalization also allows for real-time communication, so customers can get answers to their questions more quickly. These factors combine to create a better overall customer experience, which leads to increased customer satisfaction and loyalty. 3- **Better way to collect and use data**

Digitalization allows for better collection and use of data by providing access to vast amounts of information that can be analyzed quickly and accurately. With digital tools, data can be easily collected, stored, and analyzed, providing valuable insights into customer behavior, business performance, and market trends. This information can then be used to inform decisions, improve processes, and drive business growth. The result is better data-driven decision making, which leads to improved outcomes and increased success.

4- Easier to work with others

It makes it easier to work with others by providing tools for real-time communication and collaboration. With digital tools, teams can work together from anywhere, in real-time, to achieve common goals. This eliminates the need for in-person meetings and reduces the time required for manual coordination. Digital tools also allow for easy sharing of information and files, so everyone has access to the most up-to-date information. The result is improved teamwork and better collaboration, which leads to better outcomes and increased success.

5- Information and services are easier to access

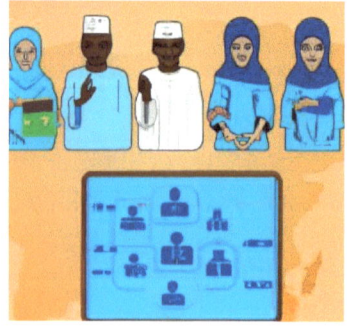

With digitalization, information and services are easier to access because they are available online. This makes things more convenient for individuals and businesses. For example, customers can now easily access product information, make purchases, and track their orders online. Businesses can also use digital tools to provide support, answer questions, and handle customer inquiries. This increased accessibility leads to a better overall experience for everyone involved.

• Chapter 2

How Digitalization changes business

1-
Business work differently:

Digitalization changes the way businesses work by providing new tools and processes to improve efficiency and productivity. With digital tools, businesses can automate tasks, streamline processes, and access vast amounts of data to inform decisions. Digitalization also allows for remote work and real-time collaboration, which improves teamwork and reduces the time required for manual coordination. The result is a more efficient and productive work environment, which leads to better outcomes and increased success.

2-
Business become more successful:

Digitalization helps businesses become more successful by improving efficiency and productivity, providing access to valuable data, and allowing for better customer experiences. With digital tools, businesses can automate tasks, streamline processes, and access real-time information to inform decisions. Digitalization also enables remote work and real-time collaboration, improving teamwork and reducing the time required for manual coordination. These factors combine to create a more effective and successful business environment, leading to improved outcomes and increased success.

3-
Businesses make more money:

Businesses make more money with digitalization because it helps improve efficiency, increase productivity, and provide access to valuable data. Digital tools allow businesses to automate tasks, streamline processes, and make better-informed decisions. This leads to reduced costs, increased productivity, and improved customer experiences. As a result, businesses can increase their revenue, attract more customers, and become more successful overall.

4-
Businesses run smoother:

Digitalization makes businesses run smoother by providing tools to automate tasks, streamline processes, and access real-time information. With digital tools, businesses can reduce manual effort, improve teamwork and collaboration, and make betterinformed decisions. Digitalization also enables remote work and real-time communication, improving the flow of information and reducing the time required for manual coordination. The result is a more efficient and effective work environment, leading to smoother operations and improved outcomes.

5-
Business become more creative and more flexible:

Digitalization can make businesses more creative and flexible by providing access to new tools and technologies, and enabling new ways of working. With digital tools, businesses can experiment with new processes, analyze data in real-time, and make informed decisions. Digitalization also enables remote work, which allows businesses to tap into a wider pool of talent, and improves collaboration and teamwork. This combination of technology, data, and flexibility leads to a more innovative and adaptable business environment, where new ideas and approaches can be easily tried and implemented. The result is increased creativity and improved business outcomes.

• Chapter 3

Using Digitalization

in your business or

group 1-Make A

plan for using

digital tools.

Here's a simple plan for using digital tools:
a- **Identify goals:** What do you want to achieve with digital tools? b- **Research options:** Look for digital tools that can help you reach your goals. c- **Implement tools:** Choose the right tools and train your team on how to use them. d- **Monitor and adjust:** Regularly check how the tools are being used and make changes if needed.
e- **Continuously improve:** Keep looking for new ways to use digital tools and adopt new tools as they become available.
By following this plan, you can ensure your business is effectively using digital tools to improve productivity, efficiency, and success.

2-Find a part of your business that can be improved by digitalization. There are many parts of a business that can be improved through digitalization. Here are a few examples: a- **Communication:** Digital tools can improve communication within a team and with customers, by providing real-time access to information and enabling remote work. b- **Customer experience:** Digital tools can be used to gather customer feedback and analyze data, leading to improved customer satisfaction and increased loyalty.

c- **Data management:** Digital tools can automate data entry, storage, and analysis, reducing manual effort and improving data accuracy.

d- **Sales and marketing:** Digital tools can be used to automate sales and marketing processes, and gather real-time insights into customer behavior and preferences.

e-

Productivity: Digital tools can automate repetitive tasks, streamline processes, and provide real-time access to information, leading to improved productivity and efficiency. By identifying which part of your business you want to improve and then using digital tools to achieve your goals, you can drive business success and growth.

3-
Start using Digital tools
a- Identify your goals b- Research tools c- Choose the right one d- Get trained e- Start using

**4-
Make sure everyone is on board with the digitalization.**

Getting everyone on board with digitalization can be crucial for its success. Here are a few tips to help ensure that everyone is on board:

a-
Communicate the benefits: Explain how digitalization will improve the business and the individual's work, making it easier and more efficient.

b-
Involve everyone: Encourage all team members to get involved in the process and provide their input on what tools to use and how they should be used.

c-

Provide training: Ensure that everyone has the necessary training to use the digital tools effectively.

d-

Lead by example: Model the behavior you want to see by using the digital tools yourself and demonstrating their benefits.

e-

Address concerns: Listen to any concerns that team members may have and address them in a constructive manner.

f-

Celebrate successes: Highlight the successes achieved through digitalization and recognize the efforts of the team.

By following these steps, you can help ensure that everyone is on board with digitalization, leading to a more successful adoption of these tools.

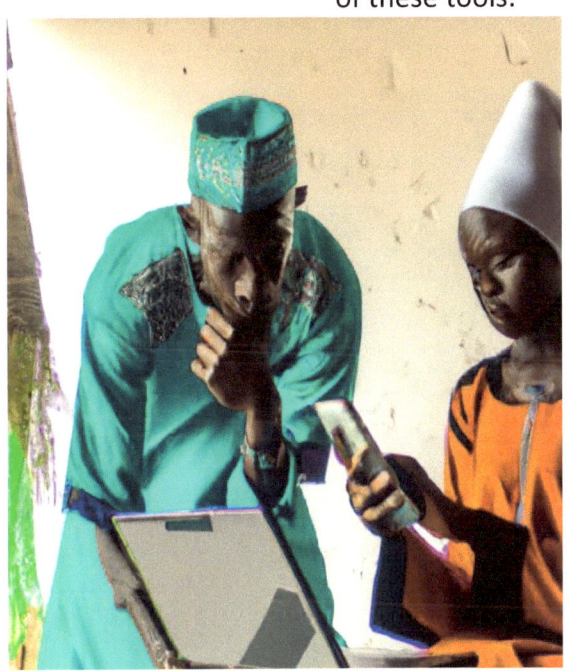

5- Help people adjust to the changes

To help people adjust to the changes brought by digitalization: a- **Be supportive:** Be understanding and offer support to those who may need help adapting to the new tools and processes.

b-

Encourage learning: Encourage learning and continuous improvement by providing resources and opportunities for growth.

c-

Provide feedback: Regularly provide feedback and recognize progress to help people feel confident and motivated.

d-

Foster a positive culture: Foster a positive, inclusive culture that values collaboration, experimentation and continuous improvement.

By following these steps, you can help ease the transition and create a positive and supportive environment for digital adoption.

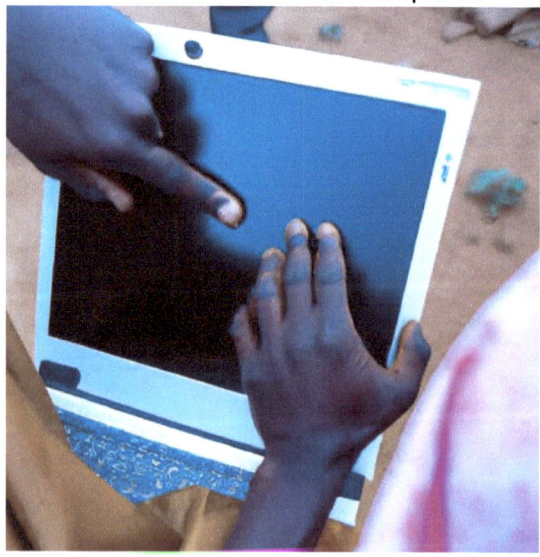

• Chapter 4

Real-life example of digitalization
1- Big companies

Here are a few examples of big companies that have embraced digitalization:

a-
Amazon: Amazon is a prime example of a company that has transformed its business through digitalization. From its early days as an online bookstore, it has now become one of the largest e-commerce companies in the world, offering a wide range of products and services online.

b-
Google: Google is another example of a company that has harnessed the power of digitalization. Its search engine, advertising platform, and other digital tools have transformed the way we access information and connect with others.

c-

Apple: Apple is a leader in digital technology and design, known for its innovative products and services such as the iPhone, iPad, and Mac. The company has used digitalization to revolutionize the way we interact with technology.

d-
Uber: Uber is a transportation company that has embraced digitalization to disrupt the traditional taxi industry. By using a digital platform to connect riders with drivers, Uber has made transportation more convenient and accessible for millions of people around the world. e- **Netflix:** Netflix is a streaming service that has transformed the entertainment industry by allowing customers to watch their favorite shows and movies on demand. By leveraging digital technology, Netflix has disrupted the traditional television and movie rental businesses. These are just a few examples of big companies that have embraced digitalization to improve their products and services, and stay ahead of the competition.

With regard to Nigeria as case-study, Here are a few examples of Nigerian-owned big companies that have embraced digitalization:

a-
Jumia: Jumia is an online shopping platform that was founded in Nigeria in 2012. It has since expanded to several other African countries and become one of the largest ecommerce companies in Africa. Jumia has leveraged digital technology to make shopping easier and more convenient for customers.

b-
Paystack: Paystack is a payment processing company that was founded in Nigeria in 2015. It provides a simple and secure way for businesses to accept payments online, using digital tools like mobile money and credit/debit cards. Paystack has transformed the way businesses in Nigeria and other African countries process payments. c- **Andela:** Andela is a tech talent development company that was founded in Nigeria in 2014. It provides a platform for top tech talent in Africa to connect with global companies and build their skills. Andela has leveraged digital technology to bridge the gap between African tech talent and the global tech industry. d- **TradeDepot:** TradeDepot is a wholesale marketplace for small retailers in Africa. Founded in Nigeria in 2016, it provides a platform for small retailers to access wholesale prices and products from suppliers, using digital tools like mobile apps and e-wallets. TradeDepot has transformed the way small retailers in Africa do business.

e- **Flutterwave:** Flutterwave is a payment technology company that was founded In Nigeria in 2016. It provides a platform for businesses to process payments, send and receive money, and manage their finances, using digital tools like mobile apps and ewallets. Flutterwave has transformed the way businesses in Africa process and manage payments.

These are just a few examples of Nigerian-owned big companies that have embraced digitalization to improve their products and services, and stay ahead of the competition. **2- Small businesses**

Examples of small businesses that have adopted digitalization include: a- **Nigerian online clothing** store that uses a website to sell their products and accepts payments through online platforms.

b-
A small restaurant in Nigeria that uses social media to advertise their menu and take
online orders.

c-
A local bakery in Nigeria that uses a mobile app to allow customers to place orders and pay for them easily.
These small businesses have successfully adopted digital tools to improve their operations and reach more customers. These case studies can serve as inspiration for other small businesses looking to improve through digitalization.

3- Group that help people

Organizations that help people adopt digitalization include:

a- **Government agencies** that provide training and resources for businesses to adopt digital tools. b- **Non-profit organizations** that offer free or low-cost technology training and support.

c- **Private companies** that offer consulting and implementation services for businesses to adopt digitalization.

These groups help individuals and businesses make the transition to digitalization, providing education and support along the way.

4- Government offices

Here are some examples from different regions: a- **In Asia**, the Indian government has implemented a digital platform called "Digital India" to provide citizens with online access to government services, such as healthcare and education.

b- **In Europe**, the Finnish government has developed a digital platform for citizens to access services such as healthcare, education, and tax returns, greatly improving the efficiency of government services.

C- **In the United States**, the state of Ohio has developed a platform for citizens to access government services, such as paying taxes and renewing licenses, online. d- **In Africa,** the South African government has implemented a digital platform called "eGovernment" to provide citizens with online access to government services, such as applying for a passport or a driving license.

These are just a few examples of how governments in different regions are using digitalization to improve the delivery of services to citizen.

5- Some of Nigerian government institution that adopt digitalization.
Some Nigerian government institutions that have adopted digitalization include:

a- **Federal Inland Revenue Service (FIRS),** b- **National Identity Management Commission (NIMC),** under FMCDE. c- **National Examination Council (NECO),** d- **Central Bank of Nigeria (CBN).**
Despite Federal Ministry Of Communication and Digital Economy that it's the Pioneer in developing and initializing it.

• Chapter 5

Problems and Risks With Digitalization

1- Safety and privacy

Safety and privacy are important aspects of digitalization. To ensure safety, it is important to use secure passwords, keep software updated, and be cautious when sharing personal information online. To protect privacy, individuals should be aware of the data that is being collected about them and have control over how it is used. Companies should have transparent privacy policies and secure systems to protect customer data.

2- Technical difficulties

Technical difficulties can arise when adopting digitalization. Some common challenges include: lack of technical skills, outdated technology, compatibility issues, and slow or unreliable internet connections. To overcome these difficulties, it may be necessary to invest in training, upgrading equipment, and improving infrastructure. It is also important to have a support system in place to help resolve technical problems quickly and effectively.

3- People don't like change

People may resist change when adopting digitalization. Some may be afraid of new technology or feel overwhelmed by the learning process. Others may simply prefer traditional methods and feel comfortable with what they know. To address these concerns, it is important to provide clear communication, training and support, and to show people the benefits of the change. Encouraging collaboration, involving people in the transition process, and creating opportunities for feedback can also help ease resistance to change.

4- Finding and keeping good digital workers

Finding and keeping skilled employees who can help you use digital technology effectively can be challenging. It's important to invest time and resources into finding the right people, and then giving them the support and training they need to succeed. This can involve looking for individuals who have experience and knowledge in areas like software development, data analysis, or online marketing, as well as those who are comfortable with new technology and willing to learn. Once you've found the right people, it's also important to provide ongoing training and support to help them grow and develop in their roles, and to keep them motivated and engaged in your company's mission.

• Conclusion

1- The future of digitalization

In conclusion, the future of digitalization is bright and holds a lot of promise. With advancements in technology and increased adoption, digital tools and processes will continue to revolutionize the way businesses operate and offer new opportunities for growth and success. The benefits of digitalization are clear and more organizations will continue to embrace it in the years to come.

2- Keep learning and adapting

"Continuous learning and adaptation" is important for staying ahead in the ever-evolving digital landscape. It means regularly updating skills and knowledge to stay current with technology advancements and changing trends. This way, businesses and individuals can continuously improve their use of digital tools and make the most of the opportunities they offer.

3- Final thoughts and suggestions

In conclusion, digitalization is becoming increasingly important for businesses of all sizes and across all industries. While there are many benefits of adopting digital tools, there are also some challenges and obstacles to overcome. It is crucial to have a plan for using digital tools, get everyone on board, help people adjust to the changes, and keep learning and adapting. In terms of technical difficulties, it is important to be prepared for potential issues and have a support system in place to address them. Additionally, there may be privacy and security concerns that need to be addressed, so it is important to stay informed and upto-date on best practices.

Another important factor to consider is the challenge of finding and retaining digital talent. As the demand for digital skills increases, it is important for businesses to have strategies in place to attract and retain skilled digital workers. This could include offering training and development opportunities, creating a supportive work environment, and offering competitive compensation and benefits.

In summary, the future of digitalization looks bright, but it is important to approach it with a plan, be prepared for challenges, and stay open to learning and adapting. With the right strategies in place, businesses can reap the many benefits of digitalization and stay ahead in an ever-changing technological landscape.

All images credit: DALL-E OpenAI

www.ingramcontent.com/pod-product-compliance
Lightning Source LLC
Chambersburg PA
CBHW040303220526
45473CB00002B/568